PRAISE FOR *RIVEI*

"Cody Smith's *River Hymnal* is a moving and absorbing book about what you can't unrun, a book that asks whether anything in our hard human world 'can return to what it was.' A hymnal collects praise, and Smith's water-haunted collection praises fractured geographies that become whole and holy in the telling. He praises working people, who come home with the smell of oil and sawdust on their hands, who know hardship, and with it an astonishing depth of hope that these poems plumb with exquisite and transportive attention. The book's varied locales are vibrantly detailed, particularly Smith's south—alive with grit and gumbo and the fierce ties of family, and rich with the beauty of loblolly pines and mallards, of river boats and 'spider legs of lightning tripping across the delta.' *River Hymnal* is a much-needed praise song for the unexpected and urgent grace of how we make our everyday lives and living, and still hold space for love."

— CORRIE WILLIAMSON, author of *The River Where You Forgot My Name*

"Oh, the holiness of rivers, of poems deep into rivers, of these poems by Cody Smith— I read them along the Metolius, along the Marys, I read them looking not for answers but for the best questions. Here's another man reckoning fatherhood and class and inheritance, another man in love with his children and his wife and the good, hard, going-away days."

— JOE WILKINS, author of *Thieve* and *When We Were Birds*

"Cody Smith's poems don't gloss over a wide stretch of river, and they don't shy away from the whole-bellied grief and lushness of human experience. *River Hymnal* takes us from Louisiana to Montana, then back south to Florida, all the while building a definition of family through great loss and cautious, spindrift hope. There are two driving familial forces in this book: the grandfather, for whom much of the collection serves as elegy, and the speaker's wife and children. I've been waiting for this book ever since finishing Smith's first collection, and his follow-up does not disappoint. Smith's vision of the South is one rich with family, labor, sorrow, and love. I want to live in this book's world of gumbo and jon boats and rivers indefinite."

— ANDREW HEMMERT, author of *Sawgrass Sky*

"The very best of our natural world informs every line of Cody Smith's *River Hymnal*. Wood ducks, still waters, expansive fields off riverbanks, baseball diamonds—These images float in the air like smoke from a fine cigar long after the poems are put down."

—JACK B. BEDELL, 2017–2019 Louisiana Poet Laureate

RIVER
HYMNAL

RIVER HYMNAL

POEMS

CODY SMITH

The Sabine Series in Literature

TRP: THE UNIVERSITY PRESS OF SHSU
HUNTSVILLE, TEXAS 77341

Library of Congress Cataloging-in-Publication Data

Names: Smith, Cody, author.
Title: River hymnal : poems / Cody Smith.
Other titles: Sabine series in literature.
Description: First edition. | Huntsville : TRP: The University Press of
SHSU, [2025] | Series: The Sabine series in literature
Identifiers: LCCN 2024018660 (print) | LCCN 2024018661 (ebook) | ISBN
9781680034080 (trade paperback) | ISBN 9781680034097 (ebook)
Subjects: LCSH: Rivers--Louisiana--Poetry. | Rivers--Washington
(State)--Poetry. | Rivers--Florida--Poetry. | LCGFT: Autobiographical
poetry. | Nature poetry. | Ecopoetry.
Classification: LCC PS3619.M5733 R58 2025 (print) | LCC PS3619.M5733
(ebook) | DDC 811/.6--dc23/eng/20240429
LC record available at https://lccn.loc.gov/2024018660
LC ebook record available at https://lccn.loc.gov/2024018661

FIRST EDITION

Cover art by iStock | AV-photo and Rouzes
Author photo by Nichole Smith

Cover design by Cody Gates, Happenstance Type-O-Rama
Interior design by Maureen Forys, Happenstance Type-O-Rama

Printed and bound in the United States of America

TRP: The University Press of SHSU
Huntsville, Texas 77341
texasreviewpress.org

THE SABINE SERIES IN LITERATURE

Series Editor: J. Bruce Fuller

The Sabine Series in Literature highlights work by authors born in or working in Eastern Texas and/or Louisiana. There are no thematic restrictions; TRP seeks the best writing possible by authors from this unique region of the American South.

*Know that rivers
end and never end, lose and never lose
their famous names*
—RICHARD HUGO

What the river says, that is what I say
—WILLIAM STAFFORD

*Said the river: imagine everything you
can imagine, then keep on going*
—MARY OLIVER

CONTENTS

1
HEADWATERS

2
TRIBUTARIES

3
DELTA

4
VAPORS

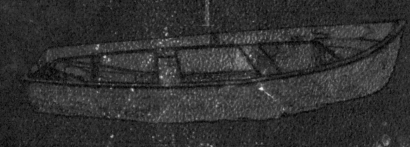

HEADWATERS

Driving from Spokane to Baton Rouge,
I Remember Rivers Cut off by the Continental Divide

Bienvenue en Louisiane, to this Lower Mississippi River Valley,
      to these parishes that swallow all this refuse the river coughs
back up. It is dark here in the Northwest like it is there. In the dream of you
      those flames still surge up factory flare stacks roasting

the southern night, and pumpjacks go on clacking their oil
      songs. But years streak over our eyes like road grime.
We are left feeling the collision of pollen and humidity
      against our faces, smelling the pines' attempt to wash

the air of big-rig exhaust between sugarcane fields and chemical
      refineries. I am not a river, even if I current down this land
to you, even if I bring huckleberries into the jasmine bush.
      In another dream this land has lost its appetite,

and I am bogged down in bayou waist-high with the cypress
      knees. I do not move. I remember being known. I hug back
that which wraps itself around my neck. Everything I touch
      is like a handshake that lasts too long.

A Friend Tells Me His Grandfather Is Dying as I Write a Note to Jonathan Johnson about His Latest Memoir

FOR ZACH JOHNSTON

And it came to pass, when they were gone over, that Elijah
said unto Elisha, Ask what I shall do for thee, before I be
taken away from thee. And Elisha said, I pray thee, let
a double portion of thy spirit be upon me. —*2 Kings 2:9*

Jon, those golden bricks of larch leaves must've already fallen
    toward you like fire-mist off the Idaho Selkirks, and I'm thinking
if I knew my life's exact happiest moment, I couldn't bear such grief.
Two years living in Spokane, my family only lost power once:
Those short days in that North country, nights with no juice
    in the lines, just the family shadows in a waltz in the living room,
just the stories Thatcher spun above the fading crackle
of Douglas fir falling to cinders, to ashes. His voice lisped
with the newness of words, the pleasure of *F*'s and *M*'s,
    long vowels lost between his teething gums. Where did that voice
go, Jon? I couldn't sleep the night he first learned his *K* sound,
him teetering circles in front of the couch chanting *Cody,*
Cody, Daddy Cody, burying forever the *Tody* which he for so long
    called me by. He wants to be a drummer, like I too once was.
Last night, he was Phil Collins walloping moving boxes
for a half hour, and I knew then that time is only mallards
circling the reeds and cypress stumps, looking for a familiar place
    to light. My friend, who is losing his Grandpa back to the clods
of red clay, called me asking what I wish I'd told my own Grandpa
as he passed. *You love him,* I said. *Who can ask for more? Just hold his hand.*
So often the only love I pass on is some thought I think later
    and with no one to tell, like this morning alone drinking coffee
under a thunderstorm that looks to rest in place a while.

What I didn't tell my friend is what I know now: before he goes,
ask for a double portion of his spirit, which is something
    I'm only saying this morning to my own dead grandfather.
And even still he comes to me now to laugh and say,
Awe, Hell. You don't want a double of this, son, his laugh
falling off like a voice carrying farther than it should
    over river water before it finally falls back into the current.

With Time and Distance, the Ledger Turns to Mist

This Northwest coffee shop smells like Pitkin,
Louisiana this morning. Is it the town's logging
industry? Those kilns that fade into winter sleet?
I look up from the stack of student essays half expecting
my logger Uncle Goodwrench to walk through the door,
but I know he's never seen a place that sells coffee
he can't pronounce. I know he's had his cup already,
the bacon sizzling the skillet, the coffee maker puffing
steam from its lid, him stooped over the sink watching
his hair gray in the window, hours before the sunrise
can backlight the pane. But that's not the smell, nor is it
a two-gallon can of gas mixed with oil, the bench seat
of his 82 Ford marinated in sweat, sawdust chips
between its cushions. It's not the smell of collard greens
and cornbread on the stove those afternoons his son
and I loaded chunks of cow patties into our slingshots.
It's not the almond croissant at the table beside me, not
the caffeinated steam gliding up from this Americano.
Out the window, a Peterbilt stops at the red light.
A screwdriver hammered into its longest log
stabs a strip of orange flagging that the wind
slaps away from me. And in this sunless morning,
I can't know in what direction.

Bowl and Pitcher State Park, Spokane, Washington

FOR THATCHER SMITH

A father leads a child to the water to grab stones to toss into the current. Ripples speed faster than the father imagined off toward the riverbank. *That's good*, he says. *Do it again. Wow*, he says. *Do it again. One more time?*

River Elegy Falling from the Wrong Side of the Continental Divide

For two years, the great Northwest and I
tried to make it work like the spouses
    of best friends with little else in common.
        I never learned its language of snow, how

it melted into ire raging down the mountain,
everything too shallow to baptize. I told that river
    about my swamp water, about sea level,
        oxbows and locks and dams, levee pumps

and flood lines, but that river could never understand it.
In a poem for James Wright, Hugo says
    a town needs a river to forgive it, and it helped
        me understand my own people, us river rats

who live in houseboats, build shacks to float
in the backwater on empty fifty-gallon drums, who make a living
    running trotlines and catfish traps, who swim
        the current in the day and let the snakes

and gators have it at night. My Red River,
Old River, my Pearl and Ouachita,
    my Atchafalaya, even James Wright's Ohio feeds
        the Mississippi leveed just across the road

from my mother's house north of Plaquemine,
cut off from me for so long by a run of mountains. In Spokane,
    I was stubborn enough to bring what I am to the river, would drive
        down South Hill past the steam plant stacks and REI outfitters,

past the meth shacks north of the city
where people wore scabbed skin
        like the flaking paint of their flophouses,
            all the way down to where the Little Spokane River spoons itself

        into its host, how I would stand over a suspension bridge
and ask that river to talk slower. Even if it was listening,
        it never heard me as it roiled over boulders fallen
            from the foothills, the spray of white water almost

        thick enough to christen my child.
Two years of this, then my leaving.
Just before the Continental Divide, I stopped
            at Hugo's Clark Fork River as if to let him

        know I gave the West a real go, then I got back
into the vehicle, climbed against the current beside the road
        up the mountain looking for my turn, to finally fall
            back down, rolling always toward the Gulf.

Flying to See My Father after the Semester's End

The magnolia looks out of place among red bay,
        hickories, & river birch, its green leaves hardening
into contrast where so much of this bottom
    drowns in drizzle, smothered by December's fog
& geese song. Everything here comes to suffer
        our touch: orange logging flags flaccid & knotted
around butternut, black cherry, & red alder,
    or else hunting lanes bush-hogged, rye grass
planted in hopes of bagging a white-tail buck
        to eat through winter. Even rain doesn't want to fall
here. It catches hold of limbs or the season's last
    leaves, prays against wind it knows will come.
I can't save it from this. Look, they will bury me there,
        though so much of my life is so far away.

Sometimes Idaho Isn't Unlike Jazz

FOR JONATHAN JOHNSON

They're both better when someone shows you how
to love them, and so we took a Saturday to cut
a rick of wood, the two of us driving up to Sandpoint
from Spokane in my wife's Mazda, a chainsaw in the trunk
wrapped in dirty clothes. He pointed from the passenger seat
toward his memories just off the road: *this is the logger
bar where I'd write. This is the land I wanted to buy when I was kid.*

When the red suspenders are pulled over the shoulders,
it's time to work, and we took turns with the chainsaw
and wood maul. I fell into a rhythm, whistling
when the roll is called up yonder even though
the two-stroke engine swallowed the tune. The whop
of the wood maul shook the veins of my arms;
the weight of the chainsaw pulled apart my back.

When the sun threatened to drop, an October wind chilled
my clothes wet with sweat. Just before we lost the light,
we walked up the tram to the cabin he built for him and Amy
to raise a daughter by candlelight. We walked the field
to stand on a rock, to hold open the barbwire fence
for each other on our way to the ridge.
Everything my hands touched, his hands had held in time, too.

Sawdust in my beard, in his long hair,
sawdust in the laces of our boots. We shook
what there was to shake and drove back
home trying to remember poems.

He told me once that everything's an elegy,
and I'll tell you, reader, that it's true,
that our own love quickens the leaving.
That night heading home, lights in the valley snuck up
before I remembered William Stafford's poem about rivers.

When I think of Idaho now, I think of diesel fumes
stirring the smell of wet evergreens, the blaze
of larch on the mountains; I think of the grit
of sawdust rubbing my heels raw,
the high cheatgrass scratching my palms,
the sugary ammonia of sweat-soaked shirts dried
in the dusk breeze carrying chimney smoke.

Nic and I burned through the wood that winter
and left the Northwest after two years
taking nothing with us except a few books and pictures,
baby clothes to keep in a box. I stuffed into the trunk
the last log he and I cut and drove it down
to the lower Mississippi River Delta,
where what little my people have kneels to rot.

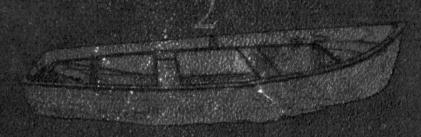

2

TRIBUTARIES

On Reading Richard Hugo Far from Home

Of course Hugo knew—like anyone knows—
    a road goes its both ways until it doesn't,
a map tells you everything and nothing.

*

My mama gave me coffee milk as a child,
    something cultural, something to make
the milk spread longer toward payday.
       I was maybe seven when I first had coffee black,
    the shock of it like a first beer. I was thirty and adrift
       in the mishap of midlife before I had it that way again.

*

That blond road turned to gray stone to black asphalt
    to red Wyoming chip seal to ice across those miles
between LaSalle Parish and the Northwest's Selkirk Mountains
       where they didn't drink bad coffee. Light roasts, dark roasts,
small batches, small farms, whole beans. And I learned to taste
       past their bitter like the molasses that hides behind
the scorch of bourbon. Pour over, Aeropress, French press,
       Chemex, water just off the boil, forty-two grams
of beans ground sand-sized to seven hundred grams
of water, all of it severe as mother stirring a roux
       for the first gumbo of autumn.

*

We teach each other vice, and it's almost
    love: tobacco, booze, old country music. None of it
is instant. I learned on the worst: Folgers and Maxwell

House. I learned to drink it at Fellowship Baptist Church,
    Shady Grove Pentecostal, LaSalle Parish Waterworks
        & Sewer District Number One, the Police Jury,
N & A Surveyors, The Belah Grocery, learned it
        on my grandparents' front porch watching cardinals
    fight the fog and each other for the killed-over June bugs
        the mosquito light zapped the night before.

                                    *

    My home's dirt road was blond. Yours, too,
        perhaps. That road isn't important. If it were,
someone would have bothered to name it,
        would have staked it proper with its green
    sign, would have battered it with a rifle shot
        from their trucks to scar that name
like the rest of our names. No, only the elder-
        dust remembers me, packed hard under
    the pea gravel and pin oak roots, if even that.

                                    *

    For three days I've read Hugo in the yard
        with the cardinals and gray squirrels
and at night to the possums and armadillos
        on their haunches rubbing their human hands
    across the sweetgum and hickory leaves
        in the woods just outside this light. He's saying
something about a blond road now derelict
        and brown as if all time is wrath. Hugo's probably right.
    Because what do I know? My father always said
        that people don't grow old being stupid,
which was something everyone I knew
        told me, a whole world converging
        to fight a child's *why?*

There is no right word for home once you've left it.
     All those words spoil under your tongue, flat and gone
long in your mouth this far on into some other life.
     There is no right word for gray, for tobacco stains
       on the front steps, coffee cups left on porch rails,
        or a yard of headstone among all the bones
that alone hold some history that even this poem's white space
         cannot say. And maybe *map* is just another word
       for grave, *home* only a taste of bad coffee scorching
        across your tongue just before you swallow it down.

Basketball Sonnet with a Wish the Game Would Go On

Even still he talks smack: *I broke them ankles; you can't*
guard me; come and get it. Things will progress, and you'll have
to really try to win. You invite him to shoot the three, give him
space to practice his handle: the crossover, the between the legs,
the jab step. He gets better: the jump shot, the layup, the floater.
More and more shots find the net. He's faster, or you're slower.

You chase him around halfcourt, his 10-year-old body darting
toward the basket. You're too tired to drive the paint, too tired to post
him up. You settle for threes, watch the high arc fall. You keep it
close to keep the game going. You let him win until one day he does
the same for you. Twenty one starts a new game until it's time for supper
and baths and help with homework, until it's time for his first job, first kiss,
first vehicle, until it's time for the first road he finds that doesn't circle back
to this town, back to this yard full of propane bottles and turned over
bicycles, his basketball's last dribble that comes to rest in the crab grass.

Thinking of Ronnie Millsap While Teaching
Freshman Composition

My students are typing self-reflections, and I'm standing
at the lectern caught between visiting professor contracts
and holding onto the air that refuses to change even this late
into October. Ronnie, it's almost quiet. It's almost like the church
that employed me once to scrape gum from pews and plunge
the johns. It must be the same quiet of the road, the big-wheel hum
over the interstate leaving some Boise casino for another small-bit
gig where they've had your face on a billboard for months.
Men I've known are catching red drum in the marsh, drinking
light beer and singing "Houston Solution" over their outdoor sinks
to the wives they didn't invite to the fishing camps. A friend told me
you lost your wife, your son, too, both of them passing on
into that always waiting other world, the one that sometimes claws back
into this one, riding to the ground hickory nuts flailing through branches
in the early evening dark. And it's almost like a song. Keatsian. Autumnal.
I haven't heard a nightingale in years, just the owl's hoot carrying over
the high-pitched Timothy slumped over by its own nightly dew. Used to,
I'd sit on the front porch at night with my mama as she smoked
Pall Malls. And there'd be crickets and tree frogs, the whole dark
grunting as it stretched over LaSalle Parish, the clacking chugs
of Justis Oil pumpjacks drumming the evening noise to pace.
And it was almost like a song, almost quiet in the way white noise
lulls. I don't know how squirrels are able to crack those hickory
nuts. I don't know how I still hear the pumpjacks' tempo. I don't
know how to lose a child, a wife, the after-image coming back
when we squeeze our eyes is the melody falling down the stairs
to me when Nic sang "Edelweiss" to our son as he fought to stay
awake those nights in Spokane when it snowed through April.
Baby Edith cooed as I sang that Dylan song about keeping her
safe from the howling winds. Do you listen to Neil Young, too?
The lyric about how only love can break our hearts? So I go on

packing mine full, ripping its seams like a pair of old britches
I can't bear to throw out. Does the music of Velcro pulling
apart our busted hearts make a minor chord? Is it almost
like a song, something we can't write? Memory lives
outside of our will like the music of a long life
we sometimes, without even knowing, hum.

Smoking in a Cigar Lounge in Clermont, Florida, I Leave with a Sonnet

Traffic plunges into the evening's gloam. We puff the afterlife
of Nicaraguan tobacco through a retro-hale. Rain splatter,
hard consonance of regret chewed back down. I want to tell
the retired roofer beside me that I came here to imagine
myself respooling those miles of interstate from Louisiana
to Washington to Florida. My beard grays. My son's voice
deepens. The years are days between a paycheck and the next run
of groceries, just cigars with a bad draw, tobacco from a pipe
smoked so fast it bites your tongue; the years are smoke
we want to hide inside the cave of our bodies so that it stays
whole until we have to let it go. The shopkeeper makes
a last call. We say our goodbyes. We ash. The gray breath
of the lives we imagined for ourselves we leave behind.

An Invitation to Say Your Wedding Vows Despite the Broken World

—FOR MICHELLE & JOE RISH

Even now the dying are born, their first feeling
    not their mother's breasts but rather the spank
of a stranger's hand against their back or foot's sole.
    Even now, the lawyers clear their voicemails, dot
        the T's and I's in what will be the erasure
    of someone's contracted promise of death
doing them part. Even now, the refugees
    flail in the Aegean Sea that will fill their lungs
while the sun warms the sand on the beach
    of Karpathos. Even now, a brother and sister
spend most of their breath arguing for the sake
    of it while a wife and husband are two ships flying
no flags as they clean their home for company
    that won't come. Even now, someone throws away
last week's lasagna. Even now, a dog pees
    on the bathroom rug. Even now, someone makes
their way past their *I do's* and into the life
    that demands they choose something they love
and hate. The mayonnaise will spoil. The hurricane
    will rip the screen door. You will raise your voice.
You will grow in your silence. You'll be too busy
    for your thirty-seventh birthday. Even now, a father loses
his wallet that held the folded note from his daughter
    that read, in misspelled words, *I lov u dady*. Even now
you know you're not the person you were at twenty
    and cannot know the person you'll be at forty. Say *yes*,
in spite of it all. Yes, while the news reports coups
    in Russia. Yes, as the earth grows its grass

across red dirt at the feet of headstones. Yes. Say it.
	And keep saying it. Because what else is there to say?
How does *no* change any of this? Say *yes*, and I will praise
	this hard world that still leaves room for my son to wrestle
me down to the rug, for my daughter to chase a butterfly
	through the bushes of still-green tomatoes, for my wife
to rub my shoulders as I stoop over the dirty dishes.
	Say yes, and I will celebrate my own love that thins
and thickens these latter days, love that is just a lizard's tail
	amputated in my garage rotting while also regenerating
the body whole like this, our life, that breaks before it blooms.

St. George Island, Florida

Sky grays far enough out into the Gulf that clouds
could be water, water could be sky. A daughter, not yet
one, sits on his lap half in water. The bloated carcass
of her diaper falls out of the polka dot swimsuit.
A son braves a few more steps, water now
to his waist, yells *I'm not afraid!* then fails
to outrun a wave to the bank. The wife
steadies herself to let the boy go
under and flail back up. Hours of salt-
water. They wrestle those kids to the truck,
eat sandwiches on the tailgate, swat away
sea birds. Driving back with everyone
else asleep, he thinks about how once
when he was sixteen, he drove Nebo Road
past Grasshopper Point where the highway
is just unmarked asphalt, blackheads of tar
that rattled his truck all the way to where the road
turns to gravel and narrows to just a lane,
until, finally, it nosedives into the Little River.
How naïve a belief: a road that could just go on.

A Poem About Leaving Home with a Bounced Check in Your Heart

I'm a sucker for old country music. Most of it
    is just common-denominator pandering, but
I listen to them twang those hometowns no one leaves
like I didn't hitch some cloud across lulled rivers
when I was first old enough to get out. I still call
    my granny who barely gets around in her hand-me-down
Monte Carlo creeping along on a spare tire
    and wore out struts to get her groceries on the days
she has enough money to eat. My mama calls
    worried about her when the checks start to bounce and tells
me the places she can no longer shop. Granddaddy died
    with twenty dollars in his billfold that I stored away
in this work desk. I listen to Kacey Musgraves sing
    about that Merry Go Round the small towners
can't escape. My students call me Dr. Smith, but I still skip
    meals, still only have enough money to put five bucks
of gas in my truck after the student loan bill hits.

Reader, I've come to learn that education
    doesn't outrun poverty any more than I've outran
my little town with its *Howdy Neighbor Day* Festival,
    its nameless roads, its dead deer strapped to the hoods of trucks
after the opening day of hunting season. EE Cummings
    once said *I am never without it(anywhere / i go,*
you go,my dear, but he was talking about carrying
    someone's heart inside his heart. Reader, I, too, carry *it*
with me, I only wish *it* was a heart and not bounced checks.
    I hang my three degrees on my office wall and sit
under them with hunger. I carry my granddaddy's
wallet. I carry checks I need people to hold

before cashing, and maybe that, too, is a kind of heart
    that my grandparents put inside of my heart, a hunger
that I drive to my temporary university job
    like the hunger my granny drives to Mac's Grocery
when the social security hits, the two of us
    hoping to outrun our names still unwritten
on the checks someone will try to cash
    after we ask them to hold it just for a while.

Sonnet for Coloring and Unemployment

—FOR MY DAUGHTER

I can't find work, and we've pulled Edith from daycare. I hurl
job applications toward places I haven't seen. A long frayed line
of my family resolve to live on that same land long enough that only a fence
will outlast our name. My daughter dresses in five shades of pink, hands me
the hairbrush and says, *make it beautiful, daddy*. I interview over Zoom
in the garage. I perform my teaching demos, tell someone else's students
that their poems can alchemize a past and future into some eternal now.
My daughter takes her time dressing dolls, invites me for tea
on the ground, pulls off her unicorn shoes, tells me, *Smell these
stinky toesy wosies*. I attempt to square a round life in some marked-through,
scribbled, labored words. My daughter toddles a box of crayons to this picnic table
to color ponies. Green grass. Purple and pink manes. She doesn't look up, taken
by her work. *Are you ready to go?* I ask. *I'm still not done coloring Applejack,*
she tells me. *It's almost beautiful, dad, just wait one more minute.*

On Not Getting You Flowers for Valentine's Day

I got groceries instead. All the hits: bread, eggs,
cereal, all the empty bags stored in the pantry. Domesticity

rages toward this midlife romance we keep sparked. I washed
the dishes, again. Picked up our children's dirty clothes,

Starburst wrappers from their own Valentine's gifts. I changed
the litter. Walked the dog. I put the onions and potatoes

away, the cheese and half and half in the fridge. The sun
was out. I rolled my sleeves under the Japanese magnolia

blooms of which I've never been able to snap a good picture.
I graded student essays, so many rhetorical analyses, page after page

of pathos, ethos, and logos. And you, what have you done today,
my love? Wake and dress little Edith and run out the door to some life

we live to be able to live together? Did your own students listen
to you today when you lectured? How long can you put off your own

grading? So much of this life is like mallards above the phragmites
quacking, circling the lake before lighting among the cattails,

so much holding, so much waiting. Last night I threw you
onto the unmade bed and kissed you before Edith could scale

the frame to butt in with her laugh that fills the room. This life
of little feet running the halls, little hands turning knobs, the sunrise

of their little voices in the halls, it teaches us
to sometimes trade making love for being in love. And I'll go on

washing the dishes and clearing the table, will go on scraping
leftovers we'll forget to eat, will go on driving us all to soccer

and baseball. And you'll go on making the bed and folding
the towels, will go on combing the kinks from Edith's long hair,

dabbing alcohol over Thatcher's bloody knees. And the house
will never be clean enough because it is lived in, because you'd

rather dance with us and read to them another book and run
your fingers through their hair that grows so fast, and I'll sing

them songs about eating their boogers, tussle with them
on the unswept floor, will bounce or kick or throw a ball.

And maybe they'll be enough of ourselves left when the day
ends so that even inside this long midlife, we'll feel young

again. Or maybe we'll feel as old as we are as we set our alarms
and warm the cold sheets into another night. I didn't get you flowers,

but some days I do, days in June and September that mean
nothing. I pass them at the end of the aisle by the freezer

of ice, a tulip bouquet, perhaps. I pick them on a whim
and spend most of the afternoon trying to find the vase stored

away in some cabinet or drawer. I love flowers because they die
so soon, love the finality of it all. And maybe I should have bought

you a dozen today, but I wanted to give you something
to outlast even us, something to stick in some junk drawer

along with the extra school photos of the kids and all the little
testaments to a long life together, the smallness of all these days

that we've left to drip like a sink overnight in some hard winter freeze,
but occasionally, we throw the faucet open and let it scald and burn.

After Not Being Able to Travel Home for the Holidays, I Sit Alone in the Garage and Watch the Rain

The holidays are hard. I haven't lost anyone
in years. This is Tallahassee, dead sweet gum balls
in the azaleas, tops of loblolly hurricane-

fractured coming to rot in the yard, Japanese
    magnolia already threatening to bloom as rain
heavies my son's basketball net. The pines

    are inflatable tube men planted in front of car
dealerships as they whip and whirl in the gusts, hurling
    cones and dead straw down. Years ago, my son fit

across my chest and grew into a toddler who loved
    those inflatable tube men. Those days I'd pick him up
from the ULM daycare after classes, and we'd stop

    and get out, and he'd touch the tube man off
HWY 165 and laugh hard enough to tremble
    his little body bleating out some language

so long now extinct. The holidays are hard, but
    I haven't lost anyone in a long time. And it's been
years since we've pumped the pills from my brother-

in-law's stomach. My father runs heavy machinery:
backhoes, trackhoes, dozers, ditch witch trenchers.
    My stepfather drives bridge pilings into rivers

with a crane. I don't have much experience with all that,
    and my hands get turned around working the levers.
My sister's friend died in the third grade. He found

his father's pistol and twirled it like Doc Holiday.
His finger caught the trigger in a revolution, and he shot
himself in the stomach. My sister's friend's dad ran

heavy machinery, too, and buried his boy alongside
his daughter whom the father buried a few years
before. And now that father has passed on from this life.

And I know the holidays are hard, and some seats
at the table are empty until more kids come to fill them.
My own children are still in their pajamas inside

playing something and being loud, their small voices
sharp enough to cut through drywall and the red birds'
chirp and the whistle of pine wind. And if this rain ever stops,

I'll take the kids into the yard to chase after leaves
that flutter toward us, and they'll catch and hold them
for a moment, will gift to them some respite from the earth

for a while in their hands, clenched and then opened again.
Waiting, I don't know why I'm thinking of my sister's
friend's dad today back in LaSalle Parish, but now

another warm Louisiana Christmas blows into the cab
of that old Chevy S-10 as I head to my then still-alive
grandparents' trailer for our holiday meal, and I pass

the field where that father buried those kids. I see him
gliding above the tracks of a dozer, one hand
fumbling the knobs, another waving at me. I think

about him covering those caskets with the last scoop
of dirt, jostling the backhoe's bucket down to pat
the mound smooth, a father tucking in children a last time.

My Daughter's Ear Infection Blues

The nurse practitioner presses the stethoscope's bulb
of plastic over your dress, and you press
                                    your face into my lung,

snot darkening this work shirt. *There, there*, she purrs
as you snort and buck. Even now
                                    the infected ear drips

dewdrops of puss. I ease my voice down into your good ear,
It's all over; you did it, love, like you could know
                                    a meaning,

like I could stop more than I can, like I could anoint you
well again with the stroke of my hand
                                    through your tangled,

wet hair stuck to your face, but today you nod and moan your sound
for *okay*, my chest cradles, swallows my heart,
                                    your tears, this tide, this ebb.

Reading Jim Harrison at My Desk in the Garage,
I Look Out the Window and Realize I've Lost Rivers

He's talking about our ability to launch without any way
to land. It's cold in Florida. Too soon, I planted the tomatoes

and bush beans in black sacks huddled in the yard.
I close the garage door to keep the gust flares

skidding across Lake Apopka out and dampen
the white noise of Fox News that my neighbor,

Lance, blares all day from his own garage. The grass
doesn't care. The wind tests the new leaves in the elms,

shimmies the STOP sign that marks this road *Virginia Cir.*
I'm lost having not seen a river in months. In Tallahassee,

my son and I would bring rod and reels under the bridge
and cast cut-up wienies soaked in packets of Jell-O

into the Ochlocknee River for catfish. Stuck in Baton Rouge
traffic jams, at the peak of Interstate-10's bridge over

the Mississippi River, I watched the tugs head up
the current on their way to the Intercoastal Canal.

There'd be fireworks on the Ouachita River July 4th.
I launched boats in washed-out landings into Old River

and Little River, ran them both into the mouth
of Catahoula Lake with people time sentenced

to memory, the day of their release unknown
knowing only that they'll one day walk free

into the swirl of wind that floats over water, wind
that understands there's no stillness in this world.

I've never gone so long without a river. My boat
derelict in the drive, waits to trigger the HOA.

The young elm leaves hold. The yard is mostly dead.
Last week, I pulled weed after weed. Yank after yank,

they gave up their roots, though in the end
there were too many. I see the now-dead shepherd's purse

and crabgrass browning, discarded on their sides.
The new weeds aren't bothered. They sway in the wind,

towering above their dead in dominion over the grass.
I'm looking for a place to land this poem about missing

rivers. I think for a moment, *grass* is the last word,
the last laugh, but it can't be. My neighbor peppers

his yard with sacks of corn for the ducks.
Mexican Whistlers, he tells me. Endangered, apparently.

They circle our homes every morning and evening.
I know that if I could only speak duck, their chirping

would tell me where they roost, would tell me of moving
water that eddies in a bend in a river that waits

for me, almost glass-still, rippled only slightly
by the softness of wind without end.

3

DELTA

Elegy with Halitosis and Underemployment as Megachurch Janitors

In this memory, I smoked with Maxine and Demarcus
          behind the baptistry door between the handicap awning
and HVAC units. I don't know why. I know I hadn't yet
          picked up the habit. Neither had Demarcus, both our hands pruned
from washing Monroe, Louisiana's business leaders' and politicians' dishes
          after the Third Thursday Luncheon. No, just Maxine smoking then,
pulling through her cracked lips and sweet onion-colored teeth
          the Palm Malls that costed her most of the day's labor.
Maxine on work leave from the halfway house, Demarcus, getting paid
          off the books, while his mother cashed his disabilities checks
at the liquor store on 4th street, how that money never made it
          to her purse, how she stuffed it into her bra, pulled it back out
in the parking lot behind the store for crack. And me, just plain poor,
          scrubbing shit from the commodes, mopping piss
from under the urinals, scrapping gum off pews, keeping the olive oil
          decanter on the alter full for anointing and leading the band
on Sundays and Wednesdays in "I'll Fly Away" for minimum wage. Maxine,
          through the halfway house work program, didn't even get that.
I don't know what Demarcus got. I don't think he knew either from week
          to week. But there we were: Demarcus with a shop broom
going down the bounds line of the church's basketball court, me behind
          him with a mop and a wheeled bucket of gray water, and Maxine
behind me riding a buffer. And we'd hope that sulfuric fog would shift
          in the wind on those Thursday Luncheons and settle over all
          those men who never looked at us, would seep into their suits
          like Drakkar Noir. But I always declined those smokes Maxine
would offer me like gas money for taking her to lunch at Wendy's
          while the three of us waited for the state van to pick her up,
how she never buckled herself in that backseat, never turned
          around. I would drive Demarcus home then,

his mother on the porch, her knees pulled up to her chin
and her rocking back and forth through the open, busted
       screen door. Damarcus would ask me to keep driving
until we made it down the block to Popeyes. He couldn't bring himself
       to ask me to buy him food, so I'd order too much
and pass the plate over, and he'd bite my biscuit and squeeze
a packet of honey directly into his mouth, his discolored teeth stabbing out
of his gums dried with blood, the stench of his breath warming
       my truck on the drive back as he kept saying, *Bless you,*
Cody. Bless you. God's going to come through for us, then got out
       of the truck and sat by his mama on the porch
and swatted flies and mosquitoes away from her arms, away
       from her cheek he would kiss before waving goodbye,
as if a front porch could be a Garden of Gethsemane,
       a buttered biscuit a Last Super, the blood from his mother's nose
sliding down her lips so that she couldn't pucker to kiss him back.

And There'd Be

Hay in the fields, hay in the barns. There'd be
        hay in flatbed trailers lugged up Tom Cat Road.

On the way to school, you might smell
        hay slunk over its bed of pasture, cow piss

on the wind. And there'd be the geese at night—
        October that passed over children's hayrides after suppers.

And there'd be the mornings your father stood
        under the kitchen lights—the loud bays of cabinets knocking

as he groped for the coffee grounds. And there'd be
        the boat ride to the duck blind: hay layered over

cypress boards, the cut pine tops squatting
        in flooded canebrakes. And there'd be hay on the backs of dogs

straying from their plywood beds under the creosote pole
        with its flood light spasms: how the dogs would beg

for duck innards as we dressed the teals, mallards,
        and gadwalls for gumbo. And there'd be the lastness of days

the dying learn to lean into—the last talk of fields,
        the last talk of tractor repair. And there'd be

your dying papaw who felt the last touch of hay dust
        when you pushed back his hair from his eyes, shook

his hand and walked away to that back pasture where cattle
        would lick blocks of salt down to nothing.

Elegy Running the River a Last Time

It's early evening and the low sun already hunkers
      heavy in the tops of loblolly past the west levee.

Grandpa says it won't rain, that the thunderheads
      are all bark. This country has seen enough, anyways,

the river up nearly ten feet and a flood of backwater
      through the tupelo and birch. I just bought Johnny Wayne's

jon boat, and Grandpa and I are going to see if the old 9.8 Mercury
      will still carry a melody of propeller thrust across

Little River. And it does. I open gun the throttle
      and the floating jalopy noses up and begins to plane

upriver looking for somewhere to run trotlines for catfish
      and turtle. Past the Army Corps of Engineers' barge

near where the river feeds Catahoula Lake, we commit
      to memory a bend with brush on both banks to come back

and tie the trotline to. But reader, this is his last ride
      and I'm throttling the Mercury again trying to plane the boat

so I can see past him and head downriver back to the landing
      as we lose the sun, and he's settling into his silence and rubbing

his hands on his pant legs and then leaning over and dipping his hands
      into the water, then up just a little into the boat spray, until finally

the burn in his back straightens him up. He rubs what's left
      of the river from his hands onto the back of his neck,

and I'm dropping the boat into neutral, and our own wake is carrying us
    toward the shore. So long without him now, this is always

the first memory: stabbing his hands out into the wind to catch
    the baseball cap flying from his head, the long gray wisps

of hair whipping across his combover, him at the front of the boat
    facing me and yelling to really crank the throttle,

and the boat tipping him above and under the horizon, always
    heading away from the landing, always upriver.

On Growing Up before the Police Jury Bothered to Name Roads Outside of Town

You've been gone long enough the scar of a clear-cut
        pine thicket has gone pink and light as skin. Now you drive
    Hanger Road back to what was home and miss the ruined woods,

loblolly, growing as fast as children, now swallowing this road.
        They've sold your horse, the one with its blazed snout of white
    against sorrel, tramping through the field to eat peppermint

from your hand, the old gelding going to glue and 4x6 pictures
        in some album to be lost. And even scars can hide in the plain
    sight of the scarred, lost to memory no one stops to remember:

the gash on your face from when you fell while building your high school's
        graduation platform, the chin bone cutting right through flesh
    now covered in beard, or the gash in your thigh from a broken beer

bottle now flush with the other flesh. You can forget a scar,
        and the wild bramble sprawl in the clearing. You can forget
    the pines and bad temper of the gelding, how he'd try to scrape

you off his back in the woods against a tree or run you into some limb.
        But remember, once, all the roads to that home had no asphalt,
    only a few other houses, four pumpjacks, three battery tanks, and no names.

Remember the smell of leather horse tack in the shed, sweet feed
        in the trough, grass hardening to hay in the field. Remember
    the easy lope through the clearing lifting you just out of the saddle,

the way the stirrups bound you to land that'll never be someone else's,
        the way it was yours just before you pulled back the reins to a trot,
    to a walk, to a dismount, to droop the saddle over a sawhorse to rot.

Duck Hunting, Hounds Jump a Deer

The morning I shot Uncle Spanky, a pair of wood ducks skirted my bank. I fired wildly into the air. The steel of my shotgun shells bombed down around him. The wood ducks flew on, but Uncle Spanky's holler skipped over the water and sunk through my skin like the BB's he was digging out of his arm with an Old Timer pocketknife. The howls of the walker hound dogs running a deer plugged the holes of my shot uncle's yelps. The roars of man and beast were ancient and moving closer. The doe hooved down my bank, flung herself into the swamp too deep for my waders, dogs baying beside me, too afraid to plunge themselves into the November water, exhausted plumes rising from the doe's wet nose like a psalm as she swam through the grove of bald tupelo cypress that Dad and Uncle Spanky had been hunting mallards and gadwalls in all morning. Uncle Spanky let her have it. Dead, the water took her down like a shipwreck of hair and organs. They waded to the spot where she went under, Uncle Spanky screaming all the while at me and the baying dogs and the deer who wouldn't die as he pleased.

Aubade Passing Home from the Waffle House

We'd been out getting as drunk as we could afford
so far from payday. Todd was letting his ponytail out,
    a dishrag thrown over his shoulder as he came from behind

    the bar out to us on the patio to make last call. I couldn't see
J's eyes, the neon lighted shamrock reflected in his glasses. I didn't
    really want to anyway. His wife was leaving, her luggage

    dragged out from under the bed, clothes stuffed and catching
in the zipper. I listened to the whole story, sipping scotch
    aged longer than their marriage. A drunk fell out of the taxi

    between the pub and Payday Loan and warbled toward us,
sometimes on two legs, sometimes on four. I'd been coming down
    for hours to drive, and I loaded J into the car. I drove us

    to the Waffle House, love bug guts splattering the windshield
as we crossed the Garden District. I ordered coffee from a booth,
    and he insisted on chocolate milk and waffles, and I slushed

    coffee into his glass when he'd look away. There's not much to say
when your wife's dragging bags down the stars to an SUV while you eat
    waffles and the happy families snore toward one another, and I kept

    kicking at J's ankles to wake him to eat. Sometime after four,
we loaded back into my car so I could drop him off to what was left. All night,
    he had talked about being a better man, about taking her dancing

    over in Shreveport, that she had asked him to once and he thought
it silly. He had lost his thought, and I looked over to see his forehead greasing
    my door window. His wife's break lights gave way to reverse

as we came up the road, and I kept driving down the block
letting him sleep once again with a body within arm's distance,
my hand out the window cutting into the dawn like a rudder.

Back Home for the Holidays, We Drive to Finch Lake

FOR CONRAD CABLE

By choice he'd hammock nights in his grandma's front yard,
        a cast open mouth's sucking snore chorusing

into the night like frog song. Getting drunk at Enoch's Pub,
        he'd say, *You don't get it, man. We're meant*

to wake up to sun on our skin, something about melatonin,
        man. Then he'd buy us another round of Manhattans.

In Manhattan, acid piqued him in Strand's poetry section,
        his face scuffing against the slender spines

of Mary Oliver and Yusef Komunyakaa, the car ride
        from Louisiana to New York weaving us

through miles of Appalachian Trail he hiked till the soup
        of dew and sweat and creek water stopped him

with trench foot. He never walked on sidewalks. *The grass,*
        man, he'd say; *our feet are made for grass, not this*

harshness. Trail preparation: Root vegetables in a juicer.
        Calisthenics up the gray-board fence still wet

with morning and grackle shit. His car is a thick waft
        of pot, frankincense, and myrrh. The Upper Ouachita

woods enclose around what headlights will catch
        of our Louisiana: the elongated mudhole that passes

for a ditch stuffed with clear-shelled crawfish, the river's levee
　　　speckled by beer cans and Little Debbie wrappers.

Everything is right: the white and black of headlights stirring
　　　a kind of dark only seen miles away from towns

with floodlights lighting people's yards. Here, loss of memory
　　　and landscape is only absence of headlights.

Driving Down I-49 from My Aunt's Funeral,
I Hope My Uncle Hasn't Relapsed

Exit 61: Turkey Creek

Last words are like overalls
        my granny hung out on the clothesline
wind-stiff, sun-faded, precarious
        dangle over bailing wire, pinned
too high for me to reach. I do not know
        what yours were, though I know
they showed you my text message, the one
        recalling you demanding the local
Barnes & Noble carry my book of poems. So much
        mediated through my grandmother,
through my mother, messages
        relayed across this assembly line
of family fastening goodbyes and proud
        of you's and thanksgivings.

Exit 40: Ville Platte

Opelousas Sostan used to come this way...I can hear
        the jukebox play, Allons avec moi, bon temps rouler.
    And soon your sister will be gone, too.
        My granny who hung all that frayed denim
on the line until it sagged like August, her humming
        gospel with a mouthful of pins, always
about some sweet by and by and finally yelling
        at me who had been riding the half empty
propane tank like a bucking bull, spurring its sides
        with my boots, the noise rattling inside

the pressurized barrel, the closed loop of a prayer's call
and response. Granny, whose a dash
of this, a pinch of that, a douse or so to taste,
left nothing the same twice, and the only lesson
in it is found so late you can hardly use it.

Exit 53: Cheneyville

Almost everyone in the ground now
lost the rhythm, the push and pull
of breath from the ventilators, but not you.
Always a paddle stroke in some other
direction from the crowd, only us gravesiders left
to worry about this new disease
they say kills your taste. I cannot imagine.
Sight and sound and smell is the way
nostalgia goes with most, but so much
of my memory is in a kitchen
fluffing rice from a microwave, hacking deer
meat tender with the side of a saucer,
dumping scorched grease in the woods,
gamy duck gumbo, peppermints
softened as it aged in its cellophane.
My grandmother, mother, my sister,
your daughters, I hugged them all anyway.
Our stories might mingle in the funeral
home's waiting room but there are no proper words
to translate what we sob.

Exit 56: Bunkie

I kept looking for Uncle Kenneth, expecting him
        to slide into a back pew. No one knows
    where he is. But fifteen years ago, you could find him
        and me at this truck stop: red bulls, diesel, boudin balls,
stretching our legs as we hauled used cars from all the Alexandria
        dealerships down to auction in Lafayette. Out of jail,
    working for himself, only wasted years and that snaggle-toothed smile
        scarred into him from a past life that stretches out
into a future we could not have known as we drove
        those ragged Monte Carlos and Ford F-150s up
    and down the loading ramp, him paying me
        whether there was work or not. His knuckles
whitening into cloudy ice as we trucked through a storm,
        his grip on the wheel as tight as an addiction.

The Fourth of July 2005

FOR NICHOLE SMITH

Nora sang "Come Away with Me" the first time we saw the sun
down and back up. I wore the week's labor thick on my skin,
sweat from bricking someone else's walls. The day had honeyed you.
Your Pentecostal hair syrup-scented from double shifts of walking
crêpes and lattes table to table. Potlucks at my apartment the Fourth
of July the days we had more friends than money. Hog in the smoker.
Burgers on the pit, drip of bacon fat flaring the ashed coals.
3 a.m. eddies all life in living rooms. We would not float there.
The Oldsmobile's windows rolled down on our way to the IHOP.
All of Monroe had hushed itself to sleep, only the occasional collision
of insect into the astral blue death of front porch bug zappers. The bayou
swamped the air. Humidity held the paper mill exhaust like a mother.
The IHOP A/C trembled our napkins. The booth window fogged
its white flag. A complete exposition of a life over pancakes and eggs:
your brother in Iraq, your graduate reading list, all the trees I felled,
the houses I built, and houses I left. Coffee cups topped off. A waitress
with tips pinned to her blouse. The shape of a face fits into cupped hands
best at 4 a.m., elbows propped on the booth, the grit of spilled sugar
exfoliating the hard skin. Windows rolled down going home.
The steal brush raked a hiss over the snare drum in harmony
with the wind. Nora sang about waking up with rain falling
on a tin roof. The electric guitar jangled. I fumbled a flat tenor.
You caught the alto. We sang for the few lit porch lights, the briars
and Bayou Desiard, for the all the life waiting past sugar cane fields,
for all the returning and for all we were still yet to leave.

To My Little Girl Who Still Doesn't Have a Name

I'm sorry. You'll be here in a few days, but your mom
and I still can't decide. Are you tired of hearing us
call you bean and peanut? The doctor called a few weeks
ago and scheduled a time to cut you away from one life
and pull you into another: January 3rd, if you hold off that long.
Dead of winter in a land of snow far from your people
who celebrate Christmas in shorts and shirtsleeves. Perhaps
we'll call you Edith after your great, great grandmother who spent
her life apart from her people, too. Or maybe Magnolia, a name
you'll be at home with if ever you make it down to the sinking
Gulf state we left. We've thought of so many things for you.
I'm sorry we're so late in deciding on a name. For so many
of your people, a good name is all they have until even it becomes
just scribbling on the back of a photograph in a box in an attic.

Watching a Video Saved to an Old Phone

It's one of those summer storms reaching for me
like my grandfather fumbling through the night
for the toilet seat, the bolts' recoil that flung
clouds, the spider web of electric current that evening
at Nic's mama's north of the parish line, my brother-in-law
out of rehab and stoned, that unlit stained glass of his eyes,
all of it filmed on my phone. We thought we were past driving
him to an ER to pump the pills from his gut, from helping him down
to bed in the guest room, from hearing him bawl over the toilet
as he tried in vain for days to piss, but it all came back in that video
where I take Thatcher to the carport away from the inquisitions
and denials to show my son the storm, to explain how the sky
can't stand the summer heat, the air already wet enough to boil
its humidity, how it all stirs up an evening shower, the granddaddy
spider legs of lightning tripping across the delta. My son's small voice
on the video demands, *Let me hold it. Let me push the budden*,
the shake of tiny hands pointing the camera toward the storm
that I argued was above us, but he knew was still just ahead.

Migration

Away from the ricks of wood, canisters
of axle grease, away from the flecking

spray painted words "ALMS FOR THE POOR"
on the LaSalle Parish dumpster on Hanger Road—

I have unanchored myself from the communion
bread packets & medicine caps of grape juice

& haven't tasted our Lord again.
Birds believe the South will be different,

that my hometown will finally plunge
down its coffins that sit mostly above ground

like acid reflux in the earth's throat.
Even now, on the other side of our old

pasture, the pines call out *red rover*
to a car-wake of wind. Today is leaving

& yet has nowhere in mind. On the front
porch my son traces the veins of leaves,

studies patterns that reveal nothing,
& crumbles them into confetti.

Where I'm from, my father rakes
these same leaves into piles

& sloshes them with gas from the mower
shed, & its smoke will soon drift back

through the widowed branches they fell from
as if a thing can return to what it was.

In the Exhaust of an Outboard Motor, I Talk to Myself and to Grandpa

If ever he were to come back to me—clawing himself up
    through a gopher tunnel from that underground city
  I know he hates, complaining of its lack of rivers
carrying catfish small enough to fry whole
    which were his favorite—he would've come to me
  yesterday when I kept asking what the hell
was the matter with my old jon boat, why
    the '69 Johnson outboard wouldn't catch its gear,
  me wheeling an Ace Hardware garbage can across
the yard to drop the propeller into, pulling a knotted
    garden hose like a leash clipped to a dog that's had enough
  walking, all in an attempt not to burn out the antique
water pump that I can't replace, that exhaust a thick wool throw
    heavy over the yard as the two-stroke motor flailed
  and spat oil across my face. And this stench from a motor
alchemizing oil and gas into a hydrocarbonic fog
    is how I remembered him smelling after hours
  of cussing clogged carburetors and watery gas, a little
catfish slime glossed across his hands, tobacco spit
    that hardened in his beard. I knew I wanted to be him—
  old-man cool banging sparkplugs with channel lock pliers,
him speaking that alien language of repair that the motor understood
    better than me. And I don't know if he ever cried
  like I've cried these past eight months when the house empties
and my own sobs that hide themselves inside these ventricles
    erupt the dam of a quiet room. I wear his boots. I wear his shirts,
  his hats. I clobber sparkplugs with pliers. I listen to his three
voicemails and answer when he asks how Nic and the kids are doing,
    how I am doing. I've just about given up on the boat,
  have nearly run out of parts to tighten and loosen as it sits

catching pollen and pine sap and straw. And maybe it'll stay
        broken down because I'm not talking repair to the boat
    but to some old man who left me six-second voicemails
and busted work boots stained in motor oil, my toes wiggling
        in the worn-out soles he fitted for me. I'll smell him
    on myself for a day, smell him in the bathroom where I'll shuck
my dirty clothes ripe with sweat and oil, and he's gone again
on laundry day, and I'm left with only the little bit of grease
and dirt under my nails just deep enough into the skin
that the clippers won't reach.

This Morning I Think of My Father's Half-Shaved Face in Shower Mist

Walking backwards, I hold his hand until he is a young man:
the smell of sweat he fed his clothes, the dirt he carried
in his brows, earth coerced by a shovel or pick axe

to let itself go. I sketch a crust of sawdust chips
in his hair hurled there by a table saw ripping red oak
and cypress, how he'd have to clean the shower of his debris

after he got out. He let me lather his face Sunday
mornings, lathering mine in return. He'd pull
a plastic Bic from a bag and slide it across my face

that knew nothing of these stubbled pock marks.
I am shaving. The safety razor pulled down my jowls,
whiskers about to clog the drain. They say you see

your father in the mirror in your own old age, but I don't
know. I'm remembering him about the time his own hair
started to speckle gray like mine. I can't see him here.

But his thumb is my thumb pulling this cheek skin tight
for the blade. Some mornings, I lean into this thumb
pulling open these pores. Some mornings, I rake away

the leaves of my body, my head tilted into the memory
of my father's blade. I pile these black and white leaves
that will not burn. If old age takes me in, let me go

inside it nearly blind, reaching for branches I have known,
the mimosa tree's long leaves over my eyes, my father's thumb
reached out to slick down my eyebrows a last time.

Last Songs

AFTER GALWAY KINNEL & ED MADDEN

What do they sing, the last birds,
the starlings that drift beyond this flooded sugarcane,
the Rorschach test of their shape shifting?

Hear the geese who have come to say
what I've unlearned.

But what do the starlings sing, flailing the wind
like water vines threading pin oak branches?

They are late evening thunderheads
rolling in while grackles gnaw the pit of their wings.

Here, walk back on this gravel passing as a road
in this low land of canebrake & flooded soy.

You can smell rain coming,
fumes from the pumpjacks.

You think you could be a raven.
You hope you're a dove.
The tupelos in the west ignite in sunset.

The geese will keep screaming.
The evening starlings are an ark
adrift in the backlit ash of cirrus.

Elegy for the Months We Lived in a Cabin Before One of the Floods

The creek had a name, though,
        I never learned it.

We were too poor for a pool,
        living for a while in that cabin
up the road from the high school.

    The water would hurt
until nearly Independence Day,
        the current cold enough to coil
a body.

        We never built a rope swing.
We were lemmings
        with farmer's tans
leaping from the tall banks.

    Sometimes, there'd be broken
bottles, snagged limbs. We learned to swim in shoes.

        We'd get out in the evenings,
ride into town with the windows down,
        wind flapping fast-food napkins
up from the floorboard,

        our hair drying
hard, textured with dirty water
        and sand.
It all flooded the spring of 2015.
    I was in Washington.

Mom in Wyoming.

>*The News Star* posted pictures online.
The twenty-foot galvanized culvert
>>that ran under HWY 556
a few yards downstream
>>from us washed out, buckling the road.

Out of frame:
>>our cabin, the azalea bush that bloomed
a few days a year but required weed eating nine months
>>>out of twelve, the potted petunias, hanging begonia bulbs,

wisteria choking the sweet gum by the porch
>>>where Scott would douse charcoal
in lighter fluid, swat the flies away
>>>from sirloins about to go on

the pit, my mother poking a wooden spoon
>>>at rock salt and ice, my sister blowing air
into an inflatable raft and wanting to tan,
>>>Nic and me almost young in a hammock.

>I can't remember the name of that creek.
>>It's not even what I think of when I think of home.

We lived light then:
>>closet floors cumbered in unpacked boxes,
ready to stay, ready to leave,
>>>water always about to rise up toward reckoning.

Aubade While Duck Hunting with My Father

It starts earlier than you think, say, 4AM, say
a father wrenching the covers off his son. It starts
in a soundless mobile home, a bag of Folgers
from the cabinet. It starts in headlights,
say, the light refracted by frost and flung
into the pine needles. It starts with the struggle
to untie the boat rope ice-hard, teeth clenching
Neoprene gloves. It starts in waves. Say
the waves sound like bike spokes slapping
a playing card in slow motion. It starts
with headlights of other trucks on the ridge
coming down Barge Landing Road. It starts
with a numb nose, stinging ears. It starts
with getting to where we're going, in the return
to quiet in the stillness of the moon-wet
water of sky, in the song of drake and hen
wood ducks whistling over, the splash of mallard
and gadwall, the smell of peanut butter crackers
on the father's breath. Let's stop time here.
Say there's as much moon-gray as flesh ribbons
on the horizon. Say a prayer for the dark to slump
over Catahoula Lake a bit longer. The day's egg
will still drop, the yoke sliming through boughs
on the embankment. Someone will always shoulder
a gun, blast after blast comes to cadence and drums
as the day marches toward you, and everything
you want to stay unfolds its wings.

The Last Year Under the Same Roof

Beavers have damned this levee I wade. My feet sweat in hip boots.
The black lab's tongue flops out the side of her mouth. I saved Coke jugs
all summer, painted them black and green, tossed them in the reeds
as decoys. I squat in the cattails. Hickory and white oaks fling their leaves.
The late October breeze rasps like sandpaper over cypress. I blow out
my lungs into a duck call. Only crows answer. The loblolly falls over
into dusk. At home, my father is clicking the lights on in his woodshed,
his hair slicked with sweat, the table saw hurling sawdust into his beard.
My mother is somewhere on Highway 8 near White Sulfur Springs.
She almost makes a U-turn before the Little River Bridge,
her knuckles sore from forcing the wheel toward home. I can hear
my father's saw ripping plywood, can hear the potholes rattle
my mother's truck in the curve past the Tingles' farm; geese are honking
above it all. I don't lift my gun. I sit and listen to all that's leaving.

Lay Him Down to Rest

FOR JOHNNY NEAL

Anyone I've ever loved enough to see them
    let down into this earth lived in LaSalle Parish
where the family is the last to see the dead.

We buried Papaw in Pritchard Cemetery
    beside his people in a new pearl snap shirt
under his bib overalls, his glasses in a soft case

stuffed in one breast pocket, a pouch of tobacco
    in the other, and I think he would've liked that,
him passing over from this life how he lived it

and only missing those two tobacco stained
    creeks on either side of his chin that the mortician
must've spent hours scrubbing off. The highway stretched

liked a clothesline of pants in the rain, and took me away
    from LaSalle, past state lines, to Washington 3,000 miles
from him in a country I couldn't explain. But the day

before he died, I had left the northwest to get another degree
    in Florida. On speaker phone with Mama at LaSalle General,
Papaw in an almost-coma, and the last throes of chronic

obstructive pulmonary disease, he shove out his mouth a vowel
    or consonant, just small wheezes of late life. I took a break
from clearing brush from the backyard, the handle of my Kaiser

blade felt as rough as a face. My little girl tugged at my overalls
    and babbled her displeasure of the dirt smeared across her hands
and knees. I told him, *Old Man, I've got nothing but work in this yard*

after that hurricane. I wish you were here to help. And it meant *Goodbye.*
    I love you, and Mama on the other end saying, *He hears you.*
He's turning his head trying to find your voice. He's so tired, Cody.

There's a picture of my mother as a child where her head
    barely punctures the shell of a puffy coat. Behind her, the trailer
is red and slashed in shadow from the sweet gum branches.

By the time I moved in with him the sun had lightened
    that red to a watered-down dose of Pepto-Bismol. Those days,
I had to beat the sun up to get to work and drank my coffee

in the dark at his kitchen table. With his combover knotted
    on top of his head like a rat nest, he joined me and asked
about the day, whether I was going to cut through a thicket

in Summerville to stake and square a drilling site for Justiss Oil,
    or off Barge Landing Road, or up near the Gator Hole
off Highway 8. He scratched his palm against his beard stubble,

coffee steam just visible in the soft stove light. He told me
    to go give my boss, Clarence, hell and come back with some jingle
in my pocket. When you're eighteen with nothing in your name

and a stack of cash behind a butter dish on top of a microwave,
     you're always walking out a front door, always more going
than coming. Those evenings, I'd pass him sitting in that Lazyboy

watching wrestling or the Atlanta Braves. He'd stop me
     as I was leaving to say, *You got your wallet?* or *those roads
are going to be slick after this rain* or *watch for drunks on 127,*

watch for hogs, watch for high water, or *check the coolant* or *check
     the oil,* or *if you run over a deer, bring that bastard home
for supper,* and all of it meant, *Goodbye. I love you.* And there

at the end inside Hixon Brothers Funeral Home as all
     the pallbearers under the awning outside stood with their hands
behind their backs, waiting, staring down at their boot toes

slipping out of their starched denim pants, I bent down
     and told him, *Well, Old Man...* and couldn't get anything out
that meant *Goodbye. I love you,* other than straightening

his suspenders over his shoulders, my hands stretched out
     for a moment like a kid reaching toward a grandfather
for another peppermint, a hand in need of something to shake.

Elegy for a Portrait Stuck on a Refrigerator of Me Holding My Son in My Cap and Gown

I'm holding Thatcher in the picture. He is three.
    He is blond hair and brown eyes and a dirty face
        smeared with strawberry Poptarts. His arm around
the back of my neck and a hand clenching the colored
    twine of regalia. My mother keeps an extra fridge
        on the back porch for frozen fish, boudin balls,
and meat pies. She hangs signs that say, *Joie de Vivre*,
    and *Why Wait for Happy Hour?* The evening sun scalds,
        lays its head down across the house tops of Sugar Mill
subdivision and tints the pond fountain the color
    of sunstruck gasoline. There's a video of my son
        in the stadium nosebleeds. My name over the P.A.,
as Thatcher yells, *Go, Daddy!* The long vowels wheezing
    out his child's lungs. My mother has the photograph
        on the spare fridge with a magnet. It faces west,
the direction of these 3,000 miles I've put between her
    and me. Feet away, Thatcher wears the body
        of an almost kindergartener. The sun sets every day,
waning bits of hue from the photograph. It is July.
    My son grows nearly too heavy to hold. In a few weeks,
        in a different corner of the country, I'll watch him
climb onto a bus that takes him from me. Soon,
    he'll fall asleep downstairs, and I won't have the strength
        to cradle him up to his room. Soon, this mold will rot
our bodies on the fridge, the sun graying our hair.

Living in the Glow of a River Boat Casino

Where we lived, everything required crossing water:
grocery shopping, university classes, following 61 down
to Baton Rouge crawling over the Mississippi every few hours.
We lived on the levee then, our bedroom window
upstairs level with the crest line, the apartments
with the antebellum columns and live oaks in the pavilion.
Our basset hound sniffed the trampled path of buffalo grass
as I helped my pregnant wife up the Ouachita River levee.
We walked the sun down talking post-structuralism
and Baudrillard; we talked in broken French;
we talked about putting a dryer on layaway or just stringing
a clothesline across the dining room. The Ouachita River
beside us loped across the delta to the Mississippi.
Sometimes the sun set just right, the ribbed sailor sky
low and soft, the smoldering day's end backlighting
the dogwood and magnolias, the hummingbirds settling
in the wild honeysuckle. Those days the dog and Nic and our
unborn son and I would sit on the levee. I would pick black
seeds off the Bahia, smell the hibiscus blooms colliding
into the sour duckweed in the backwater. We knew we were leaving
and dreamed of ways to stay, to man a houseboat downstream
in the wake of a river boat casino captain asleep at the wheel,
to nightfish in its glow. If we were leaving, we'd take what there was
to take as the tree frogs and crickets and buzz of mosquitoes overtook
whatever we had to say, the vehicle lights behind us leading home,
the bow light from a boat upriver leading somewhere else.

Walking My Grandfather's Garden Gone to Weeds

Feel tomorrow like I feel today,
I'll pack my trunk, make ma git away.
—St. Louis Blues

That black dirt mattered those days
      when there was someone tending it,
   hoeing weeds, disking gnarled clods back

to the surface. Blight cost something. We'd pick
      before dusk, him singing *I hate to see*
   that evening sun go down, a bushel of peas gathered,

a five-gallon bucket of yellow squash dangling
      from his hand, raking across the leg
   of his fouled overalls. Summer money mattered,

him bear-hugging mayhew trees, shaking down berries
      onto a bedsheet I spread out under its limbs,
   bringing that bounty home to make jelly

we'd sell by the jar. We could smell rain coming as it doused
      all the dirt roads of LaSalle parish, mingled
   with the exhaust of the pumpjacks and the wild wisteria

and jasmine, and that mattered, too, how the next morning
      we'd check the rain gauge threaded through
   the hurricane fence wire. He'd document

the inches and pour out the cylinder
      into a three-gallon bucket of hose water
   for the mutt yard-dog. Nothing went to waste then.

The soft mush of squirrel innards and organs,
          the hounds ate; Ma Peg would stew
     what was left, sop the juice in cornbread.

I'd watch him nap those summers
          when he'd come home from his first job
     at noon, crumbs from a tomato and mayo sandwich

on the arm of his recliner, his eyelids flopped over,
          puffs of air parting his lips. Granny would wake him
     with coffee we'd take to the porch, a clump

of chewing tobacco wadded into a ball
          on the handrail from the morning he planned
     to reuse that afternoon. Everything with its uses

and reuses. The night sky taps its dead light down
          to these fields now unworked, light with memory
     of a world that's past or to come, soft light

that can find the years' melody singing,
          feelin' tomorrow like I feel today, light that knows
     how to hold that moment in a way you almost believe.

Elegy for the Years in the Garden District with Nic

We'd walk through the last hours of day
    giving over to dusk alongside the sea-level

mountain bikers with nothing to climb but the levee
    in that river town, teens from North 3rd

and Glenmar coming to spray paint the maze and pump station
    walls. The tight rope of levee lifted us above the town

and water. Steam left behind by a summer flash rain held the sweet
    and sour waft of jasmine, gardenia, and duckweed,

the humidity gluing black bahia grass seeds to our legs. We danced
    in that kitchen in a five-hundred-dollar apartment

with a hot water heater by the stove, washing machine
    by the fridge. Remember those evenings out back

on the levee just past where the tupelo and magnolia sweetbays
    opened where we could see a mile down the river

to the next bend, how we sat there and talked over the mosquito buzz
    about moving to Tennessee, France, Oregon,

about buying a house up the road? Remember the river star
    of a boat's red light drifting down the water away

from Monroe, how we'd forget to flip the kitchen light switch off?
    Behind us, the one bulb burning, the other's blown fuse waiting

to be unscrewed, the tree frogs screaming about nightfall. Dead ends
    are hard to name. Remember being able to go anywhere?

The river was almost still enough to believe the town
    could hold it, could paint over the graffiti like it mattered.

Country Roads Aren't Always a John Denver Song

The year before my parents unwed themselves,
my father kept taking me to our hunting camp
in the Aimwell hills. I was a kid, and he was quiet,
his face hard shale or flint. Between us: our rifles,
barrels pointing down to the floorboard, Honey Buns,
Nutter Butters, bullets and shotgun shells, hunters' orange
vests. We were never more than an arm's-ength apart,
though neither of us tested that distance. Even the stars
seemed far and cold and still or like salt in the bottom
of a bowl of popcorn. Before deer season, he tied
orange flagging to trees to help me find my way. Those frost-
still mornings, he'd pull over at the creek bridge and wish
me luck as I grabbed my rifle and flashlight. One morning,
twelve years old and in the dark alone, I lost the trail.
I wandered through the hardwood hoping to find
my deer stand propped against a beechnut tree. I wandered
lost into the long first fingers of light. I walked a road
I didn't know until it ran into a road I did know. And I walked
that road until I was back at the bridge where my father left me
and waited to be found again. "Okay" and "Not much," I told my father
when he asked about my morning, when he asked about what
I had seen. In my head, I asked over and over if we could go
home. He passed me a bag of opened Cheetos, told me to eat
my breakfast. We drove most of the day alone together in the woods
down roads that I didn't want to learn, roads that would never
be given names because of where they ended.

4

VAPORS

Sonnet Beginning with Lines from Keats and Ending in Dust

When I have fears my name will live beyond
    this flesh that years will pull to vellum,
  I know yet still my children, then grown
    thick and hunkering in their late days, will read
about a son, about a daughter I held
    in these hands which they had yet let go,
  these hands like my father's saddle, broken,
    hanging from a joist in a barn only touched
by a horse-hair braided breeze heavy with hay dust,
    and I think even dew sliding from the dark
  bracken returns again even if we don't notice it,
    even if we don't care, the dust of my bones,
dust of my voice, dust on my name on a book spine
    on a shelf waiting for you, my loves.

ACKNOWLEDGMENTS

Cactus Heart: "Duck Hunting, Hounds Jump a Deer"

Chestnut Review: "Walking My Grandfather's Garden Gone to Weeds"

Fourth River: "Sometimes Idaho Isn't Unlike Jazz"

Gettysburg Review: "Country Roads Aren't Always a John Denver Song"

Jabberwock Review: "On Reading Richard Hugo Far from Home," "Thinking of Ronnie Milsap while Teaching College Composition"

Louisiana Literature: "Aubade While Duck Hunting with My Father," "The Last Year Under the Same Roof," "My Daughter's Ear Infection Blues," "Driving from Spokane to Baton Rouge, I Remember Rivers Cut Off by the Continental Divide," "To My Little Girl Who Still Doesn't Have a Name"

Puerto del Sol: "Elegy for the Years in the Garden District with Nic," "Living in the Glow of a River Boat Casino," "Elegy for the Months We Lived in a Cabin Before One of the Floods"

River Styx: "Elegy with Halitosis and Underemployment as Megachurch Janitors"

San Pedro River Review: "River Elegy Falling from the Wrong Side of the Continental Divide," "Back Home for the Holidays, We Drive to Finch Lake"

Sand Hills Review: "On Not Getting You Flowers for Valentine's Day"

The Arkansas Review: "The Fourth of July, 2005"

Sugar House: "And There'd Be"

The Florida Review: "Aubade Passing Home from the Waffle House," "Elegy Running a River the Last time"

Talon Review: "Migration"